Dawn's Early Light

Ty Wheeler

Todd Trainer

Ken Harriss

Foreword by Dr. Johnny Hunt

Copyright 2017 Ty Wheeler, Todd Trainer, and Ken Harriss
Dawn's Early Light
Published by Yawn's Publishing
2555 Marietta Hwy, Ste 103
Canton, GA 30114
www.yawnspublishing.com

All rights reserved. No part of this book may be reproduced or transmitted in any form, electronic or mechanical, including photocopying, recording, or data storage systems without the express written permission of the publisher, except for brief quotations in reviews, articles and for educational purposes.

The information in this book has been taken from various sources, and is presented with no guarantee of its accuracy. The information in this book is presented as the author intended. Yawn's Publishing assumes no liability for the accuracy of the information printed, or any information used without permission.

Library of Congress Control Number: 2017914579

ISBN: 978-1-947773-02-8

Printed in the United States

To the nearly 3,000 people who lost their lives in New York City, Washington, DC, and Pennsylvania on September 11, 2001.

"For I know the plans I have for you," declares the Lord, "plans to prosper you and not to harm you, plans to give you hope and a future."

Jeremiah 29:11

FOREWORD

I deeply love the Harriss family, the Trainer family, and the Wheeler family. They have been very involved at FBC Woodstock in many different capacities for the majority of the years I've been privileged to serve as their Pastor. These families have blessed me abundantly over the years.

Ken, Todd, and Ty are all very creative people who are using their creativity to honor the Lord in differing ways. For example, Ty is a pharmacist by profession. However, he has been greatly gifted by God to write Christian fiction. My wife Janet has loved reading other books he's published ("Phobia", "Pinpoint") and looks forward to the next one.

In this moving story, "Dawn's Early Light", these three co-writers recount in great detail, true stories and events we were all confronted with on the morning of September 11, 2001. It was one of the greatest tragedies of all time. We were all gripped by fear as we started that memorable day. Ken, Todd, and Ty were in New York City that day and were scheduled to eat breakfast atop the World Trade Center at 9:00 a.m. (the precise time that tragedy struck) the morning of the 11th, but circumstances disrupted their plans and dictated that they take an earlier flight out of New York. They would later see the providential hand of God in their activities the rest of that day and in the days that followed.

You will be saddened and yet encouraged, blessed, and challenged as you read this story that affected our entire world and see, once again, that God moves in mysterious ways in our lives. Read it and pray for our country, and pray that we will be reminded of how good God is and thank Him for His goodness and His provision like we did in the days, weeks, and months after 9/11. God, forgive us for not blessing You continually.

Dr. Johnny M. Hunt

Senior Pastor

First Baptist Church

Woodstock, Georgia

1

Every good story has to have a beginning that grabs your attention, and usually it's diametrically opposed to how the story ends. However, it doesn't have to be that way. This story isn't like that at all. This story is NOT fiction! This story is about the goodness of God in the beginning and the goodness of God at the end. As Revelation 21:6 says, "I am the Alpha and Omega, the Beginning and the End," and truer words were never spoken. God is just as good now as he was in the past and will continue to be in the future. To quote it another way, "God is good all the time, and all the time, God is good." He gets all the glory and praise, and that's why we decided to share our story---to lift up <u>His</u> name. For the moment, let's meet some of those He calls His children, the ones He loves and the ones who love Him. The ones who were the characters in this true story that only He could have been called the Author.

The year is 1996 and the city is Woodstock, Georgia. Three men are about to meet in the Renny Ryder Median Adult Sunday School Class at the First

Baptist Church of Woodstock. Ken Harriss is a native of Decatur, Georgia before moving to Woodstock in 1978 and joining the church in 1994. He is the primary owner of a successful drywall business.

Todd Trainer grew up in East Point and Palmetto, just south of Atlanta and moved to Woodstock in 1988, joining the church the next year. He is a mortgage loan originator with a firm in Marietta, Georgia.

Ty Wheeler is the final member of the trio. Born and reared in the South Georgia town of Dawson, just outside of Albany, he migrated to Woodstock in 1998 after joining the church two years prior. He is a pharmacist in Roswell, Georgia.

The Sunday School class was a rather large one, so almost everyone knew each other, but may or may not have been close friends. One would have to make a concerted effort to become better friends by hanging out outside of class or if the wives became friends, then the husbands were included by default. The other way that people became friends outside of class is if they served within the church in the same capacity. In our case, we grew to know each other better by singing in the choir, Ken in the bass section and Todd and Ty in the tenors. Choir practice was usually on a Wednesday night until 7:30 or 8:00 p.m., so we would often have dinner together afterward. All-you-can-eat chicken wings at a local restaurant near the church were usually on the menu with several guys often joining in on the feast. More often than not, there was some kind of live sports game on the TVs inside the restaurant. Usually it was the Atlanta Braves, but we didn't care much. After all, it was baseball.

One particular night, the conversation turned to the various stadiums around Major League Baseball and which stadiums were the best and worst. All of us had done enough travelling in our lives and had been to a majority of the more notable old ballparks. Fenway Park. Wrigley Field. Dodger Stadium. Busch Stadium. Shea Stadium. And of course, Atlanta-Fulton County Stadium. But there was one that glaringly stood out, one that somehow escaped a visit on our bucket list of ballparks. One that had been around since 1923. It stood at the corner of East 161st Street and River Avenue in the Bronx borough of New York City. It had undergone a huge renovation after the 1973 season until 1976, where it would reopen with a new interior, but much of the exterior looking the same. It was the one and only Yankee Stadium, home to baseball's New York Yankees. As far as stadiums and winning teams go, there is a short list of iconic teams and stadiums that can be mentioned in the same breath. In football, it was the Green Bay Packers and the frozen tundra of Lambeau Field. In basketball, it was the Boston Celtics and the Boston Garden. Hockey had the Montreal Canadians and the Forum. Without question, the Yankees and Yankee Stadium fall into that small, yet prestigious fraternity.

As the conversation continued, it appeared that surprisingly no one at the table had ever been to a game at Yankee Stadium. A lot of the guys there wanted to go, but there were only two guys that really pushed the issue. Todd and Ty had gotten a certain look in their eyes, plus had the available time to go.

Most everyone at the table had an interest in going, but for one reason or another, could not make it happen. As the group meandered out of the restaurant that evening, Todd and Ty had already mentally started putting the trip together. As they were doing so, Ken came up to them to reiterate how serious he was about going. He said that if they were dead set on going, then count him in as well. The travelling party had escalated to three, and that night into the next day, the planning would begin.

Todd had been to New York City several times before for Christmas season shopping trips and other leisure excursions, so he knew the best place to stay would be the Edison Hotel in the heart of Times Square. The mayor of New York, Rudy Giuliani had made it a point to clean up Times Square, once a dirty and unsafe part of New York City, transforming it into a much safer and family friendly destination. Todd had seen the difference first hand, so he had no qualms about where to stay.

The next step would be securing tickets. Ty had used a sports travel guide over the years to get tickets to other sporting events and to find the best possible seats. However, Todd had an even better idea. He knew that a member of our choir, Paul Mastropasqua, who sang in the bass section, was good friends with the Yankees manager Joe Torre. Paul was a former Mr. New Jersey in bodybuilding in 1972, then gravitated to a strength and conditioning coach for the New York Jets and New York Mets in the late 1970s. He also coached for the Atlanta Braves in the early 1980s before working with Torre during the 1996 and 1997 seasons until his retirement. It was always neat to see the gigantic World Series ring adorning Paul's finger. Todd was able to track down Paul soon after, and Paul indicated that getting tickets should not be a problem at all. Even after telling Paul the date we'd like to go, September 10th against the Yankees most hated rival the Boston Red Sox, he was still confident that Joe would be able to help us out.

Our trip was neatly coming together. We had the hotel secured. We had the tickets secured. Now all we had to do was get to New York City. This was the easiest part of the trip. Todd's wife, Cindy was a flight attendant for Delta Airlines and Delta had a buddy pass program. A buddy pass program was for family and friends of Delta employees and it meant that for a very nominal fee, those people could fly stand-by to a particular city, provided that the flights were not already filled with passengers paying the full fare. Those flights could be at good times or they could be at very inconvenient times. You were last in the flight hierarchy when it came to seats, so a little bit of luck was often involved, and you could be bumped off a flight at any second. After consulting with Cindy, we decided we would have better luck trying to find an early morning flight into New York, then we could do a bit of sightseeing before heading over to Yankee Stadium. We ended up on a 6:40 a.m. flight leaving Atlanta on Monday September 10th and arriving at 8:45 a.m. at New York's LaGuardia Airport. We would have plenty of time to check into the hotel, check out the sights, sounds, and tastes of New York City and maybe even squeeze in a nap before taking the D subway train out to the Bronx. The day was overcast, but we hoped we'd get in some baseball later that night. What we didn't know was that the storm was already rolling in, in more ways than one.

2

The time was drawing near, the time of year when the end of baseball season coincides with the start of football season. For the sports fan, it is an extremely busy time of year for watching, or for those fortunate enough, attending games live. The beginning of college football season normally meant that attending baseball games in person took a back seat to attending football games in person. Occasionally, there were a few exceptions to this rule. If the Atlanta Braves were in the playoffs, which they often were in the years spanning 1991 through 2005, one could be forgiven for keeping an eye on baseball or even taking in both football and baseball games live on the same day. In 1996, the University of Georgia was undergoing a difficult head coaching transition in football, and Ty took a unique opportunity to visit Wrigley Field in Chicago with his wife and friends to watch the Cubs take on the Braves. That very same day, new UGA Coach Jim Donnan lost his very first game at home to Southern Mississippi. A game at Yankee Stadium might certainly be considered an acceptable exception to the rule, but in our case, that wouldn't be necessary.

The dog days of August had bled into September, where the days were still just as blazing hot. It was a Saturday night, and UGA's brand new coach, Mark Richt, had just lost the first game in his regime's inaugural season, a narrow 14-9 decision to Lou Holtz and his South Carolina squad in Athens. Richt had taken over for the fired Donnan at the start of the 2001 season. Since Ty had attended the game and had to work the next day, and Todd was involved with a choir special that particular Sunday, we'd made our plans to fly out to New York City on Monday morning. We decided that it would be much easier to fly out with buddy passes on a Monday instead of a Sunday. We'd all been excited about going, Ken and Todd for a return trip to the Big Apple and Ty for his first ever trip there. Ken, who was part-owner of a sports memorabilia shop in Woodstock, had even brought three Yankees caps to choir the previous Wednesday for us to wear to the game. Everything was coming together, but the one thing that we were all keeping an eye on was the weather in New York City. We'd all been watching the various forecasts for New York and everyone was saying the same thing. Monday's weather was due to be overcast all day with showers and/or possible thunderstorms throughout the day. Hopefully we'd dodge the rain and manage to squeeze the game in, or at least that was our thought process as we made our way down the jet way to board the plane that would take us to LaGuardia International Airport. We had high hopes as we departed sunny Atlanta Monday morning on Delta flight 708 and landed nearly two hours later in an as-predicted overcast New York City. The morning rush hour was nearing its end, although New York City traffic is never really "over", as we hopped in a cab and made our way to Manhattan. We were still a little too early to check in at the hotel, but they were nice enough to store our bags so that we could go on a quick exploration of the Times Square area. We were able to walk over to the toy store FAO Schwartz and waste a little time there before making it to 30 Rockefeller Plaza, where the NBC Experience and Studio Tour was located. Time ticked away as we suddenly felt the pangs of hunger getting the best of us. We'd talked about places we wanted to visit and spots where we wanted to eat before leaving Atlanta, and one place that continually popped up was Carnegie Deli. Since we weren't that far away, we decided to make that our lunchtime destination. Carnegie Deli is known for its humongous portions when it comes to deli sandwiches, so we had more than enough left over as we waddled our full bellies back toward our hotel. As we walked off our sandwiches, we thought we'd check to see if our room was ready. Luckily it was, so we made our way upstairs for a short nap before doing more sightseeing and then heading out later to the Bronx for the game.

A couple of hours later, we began to stir and get ourselves ready for the main event, the thing we'd all come here to see. We'd made plans, cleared work schedules, and saved our money so that we could check off a major item from our bucket lists. A New York Yankees game at Yankee Stadium! It was going to be a great night. Or so we thought. Before we left the hotel to catch the subway, Todd and Ken checked two of the most important items of the day. First was the weather, and it hadn't appeared to change at all, still overcast and still a very good chance of rain. However, we were optimistic and were prepared in case there was a rain delay, making the game start later than normal. The game was against the Red Sox after all. They'd do everything within their power to get it in before the weather took over. Second were the flights going back to Atlanta the next day. Todd called a phone number which informed him of the number of stand-by seats left on every flight leaving LaGuardia and heading to Atlanta on Tuesday. Fortunately,, there were available seats on nearly all of the flights and at several different departure times. Since we had our pick of times to leave on Tuesday, we decided to stick around and do some more sightseeing in better weather before leaving on a late Tuesday night flight home. We all had to be back at work on Wednesday, so we were determined to make the most of the time we did have in New York City. We knew these plans could change, since flying on a buddy pass requires flexibility as far as departure times go, but right now we were looking good. Tomorrow's forecast was more promising, so it would be a great day to be a tourist. One of the places we'd decided to visit was the World Trade Center. We debated back and forth between the Trade Center and its more famous relative skyscraper, the Empire State Building, before settling on the WTC. We'd start our day with breakfast at the top of the World Trade Center, then tour more of the city before heading home that night. Todd called his wife Cindy to inform her of our plans, then we headed for our subway train.

We arrived at Yankee Stadium about 5:30 p.m., an hour and a half before the scheduled game time. Ominous clouds still hung overhead, with the random raindrop or two leaking from them. We posed for pictures outside of the stadium with the familiar white façade in the background, then decided to go inside for the pregame festivities. Making our way toward the stands, we were amazed at the beauty of Box 215, Section 3, Row B. Some of the best seats in the house, compliments of Don Zimmer, the legendary bench coach of the Yankees. Our friend Paul must've really buttered up his old pals Zimmer and Joe Torre to get us such great seats, and against the Red Sox to boot. Shortly after taking in the view, it was time to take part in the obligatory pregame ballpark food, consisting of hot dogs, peanuts, and Coca-Cola. Just as we got our food and were heading back toward our seats, the rain began to fall in earnest. At first, it fell soft and steady. Then it gradually became a deluge. The buckets of rain caused everyone in the stands to take cover from the downpour. We also found temporary shelter under one of the overhangs situated higher up toward the top of the lower level seating bowl. We could eat our dinner in peace, stay dry, and watch the rain, hoping for only a delay in the starting time for opening pitch. While we were waiting, we noticed a familiar gentleman near the seats we now occupied. Actor Jon Lovitz, who'd been a cast member of the TV show *Saturday Night Live* and had appeared in such movies as *City Slickers*, *Big*, *Three Amigos*, and *A League of Their Own* was also waiting out the storm. We introduced ourselves and as we had a quick conversation with him, he was amazed and impressed to learn that we'd flown all this way just to see a game in Yankee Stadium. We took a quick photo with him, then before we could say goodbye, the Stadium public address announcer turned on his microphone.

3

"Ladies and gentlemen, due to inclement weather in the New York City area, and with the radar indicating that more is on the way, officials with Major League Baseball and the Yankees organization have decided to postpone tonight's game."

We felt like we'd been kicked in the stomach. We had hoped that after coming so far and being so close to experiencing a "bucket list" type event that maybe they would give it a little longer before calling off the game. However, the decision was made relatively early into our time at the stadium. Well, at least we'd get to spend a little more time touring New York City before we'd have to leave, right?

The public-address announcer went on to explain how we could use our tickets as a rain check and to which of the remaining games we could use them. Since the Red Sox were a huge opponent, there was no chance of playing a doubleheader the next day, as is often the case in baseball rainouts. Unfortunately, this would not be an ideal situation for any of us, as the announcer stated that the tickets could be used for any of the few Yankees games remaining in 2001. However, they could also be used for certain selected games in 2002 as well. That tempered a little bit of our disappointment, as we knew that we probably wouldn't be able to make it back this year, but the next year would be a distinct probability. As we discussed our options, we said goodbye to Mr. Lovitz and crept our way toward the subway and out into the rainy night. On the crowded ride back to Manhattan, we decided to pick up some dessert before heading back to the hotel to discuss the next day's plans. Ken always has to have either some kind of chocolate dessert or a slice of cheesecake, so who were we to deny his sweet tooth? Once we'd finished dessert, we headed back to our hotel room. Todd had decided to check the flights on his cell phone one last time before we started making plans for the next day. When he'd checked earlier in the day, all stand-by flights were pretty much wide open for the whole day on September 11th. It was a good thing that he checked again. Within the space of a few hours (or a rained-out trip to Yankee Stadium and back) every early morning, afternoon, and evening flight had mysteriously booked solid---except for one. Delta flight 499 would be leaving LaGuardia at 9:00 a.m. the next morning for Atlanta, and it was the only flight left with available seating. Since we were flying on buddy passes, we had to go whenever there were open seats---and this was the only one! Our trip had just gone from bad to worse. First the Yankees game gets rained out and now our day of sightseeing had just gone down the tubes. It almost felt like a wasted trip, except for the awesome food and it being Ty's first ever trip to New York City. Because of the late hour and the fact that Todd's wife Cindy was often in bed early since she flew on early morning flights, he decided against calling her and letting her know of our major change in plans. No breakfast at the World Trade Center for us. Todd and Ken had both agreed that the World Trade Center was a much better view for breakfast than the Empire State Building, and now that idea was gone. We decided that we had better get to sleep pretty soon since now we would have to rise early for our taxi ride to the airport. Before we knew it, we were all asleep until the alarm the next morning shook us back to reality.

We checked out of our hotel in the early morning light and climbed into a waiting taxicab for our ride through traffic toward LaGuardia. We were bleary-eyed and lamenting the fact that we were not able to stay in New York for the day. On the taxi ride over, Todd got his wake-up call. The cab driver had apparently left his window open the night before, and Todd was left to enjoy the unseen after-effects of all the previous night's rain. The seat of his pants had gotten soaked from the wet back seat of the taxi! As we crossed the East River and looked back toward lower Manhattan, we joked about Todd's wet pants, then about how soon we could get back to New York to take in another "first ballgame in Yankee Stadium." One of us even wished aloud that we should have been lucky enough to be at the top of those twin towers right then, having that breakfast we'd planned the day before.

When we arrived at the airport, LaGuardia was its typical busy self, even that early in the morning. Our friendly gate agent checked us in, but told us our flight would leave a little later than its scheduled 9:00 a.m.-ish departure. No worries, we said. We waited in the gate area for a while until we noticed that another Atlanta-bound flight, Delta flight 2175, had open seats and was leaving from the next gate over before our revised departure time. We asked the agent if we could be moved to that flight instead. We were puzzled when we saw that his friendly demeanor was now more reserved and almost agitated. However, he did move us to the new flight and said abruptly, "I suggest you board that flight right now," and quickly looked away. We complied, but were struck by his change in attitude.

Stretching out in the open seats in row 28 on our new plane, we looked forward to the two-hour nap on the flight home. As we pushed back from the gate and began to slowly roll toward our runway, the plane suddenly stopped. We thought nothing of it, until we were startled out of our pre-nap haze by the airplane's captain. Instead of the usual departure order or weather report he would normally give before takeoff, the captain announced over the PA that a plane had struck one of the towers at the World Trade Center. With three major airports and dozens of smaller airfields nearby, Todd commented aloud that it wasn't beyond the realm of possibility that this could have happened. Some of the passengers near us began to check their phones to see if they could get any information on the accident. We were all thinking the same thing—a small private plane had crashed into a building and hopefully we'd be departing soon. The captain taxied the plane back to the gate and asked everyone to leave the plane, but to remain in the gate area for re-boarding that would begin shortly after the airline did a "quick security check."

As we walked back up the jet way, most of the passengers were wondering how a pilot could not see one of the tallest buildings in the world and manage to steer his plane clear of it. Several were still on their cell phones, trying to get updates on the situation and letting their friends and loved ones know that they might be delayed. Included in that group was a small lady who was on her way to her mom's house in

Alpharetta, Georgia to get it ready for her move and a young black woman who was anxiously speaking to someone on her cell phone, but fearing the worst-case scenario. Little did we know that we were just a couple of miles from all that was unfolding and had no idea that we could have seen it all outside the window. The news would only get worse. Much worse.

4

My mom has told me on more than one occasion that "no matter how old you are, you will always be my baby." I guess that means that no matter one's age, a parent never stops being a parent. That being said, Todd's pre-smartphone cell phone began to ring as we walked back into the gate area. He checked the caller ID and saw that it was his dad, Wendel. Todd quickly answered the phone with the question we all wanted to know.

"What in the world is going on?!"

"Son, you don't want to know," he replied. Mr. Trainer then asked Todd where he was, and suddenly realizing that he hadn't told his dad about the one-night baseball getaway, responded by saying the same thing.

"Dad, you don't want to know."

Call it parental instinct or just being a dad, but somehow, he already knew. It was more of a statement than a question.

"You're in New York."

"Yes, sir," Todd replied very weakly.

He then gets our undivided attention by making us promise that we will not get on an airplane that day. At that time, Todd's dad was also working for Delta Air Lines in flight attendant scheduling. He was not only watching live coverage of the events on television, but he was also getting real time updates from Delta. Later, he goes on to tell Todd that not one, but two planes have struck the towers, a separate plane had just crashed into the Pentagon, and that yet another plane was off the radar and unaccounted for presently. Todd asked what kind of planes and Wendel replied "big ones". He starts to choke up when he tells Todd how many people are believed to be dead. The next statement from Mr. Trainer chilled us all to the bone as Todd relayed to us what he'd been told.

"Son, we're at war."

As we began to suddenly realize the gravity of the situation, Todd went on to ask about his wife Cindy. As with any other flight attendant, one never knows for sure where their day will end or begin, and Todd remembered his wife was somewhere out there too. Mr. Trainer tells him that she is safe in Greensboro, NC and says that he will update us when possible. Moreover, he says that they've gotten word that all flights are being grounded for now.

Todd glanced up and recognized that we had a bit of an audience gathered around us as other passengers from our flight were listening to his conversation, some wide-eyed and afraid. A few are getting calls from their loved ones on their cell phones, but the cellular service is slow at best and starting to bog down. Many at the bank of pay phones are unable to get a dial tone, or if they are lucky enough to get one, they are not able to get their call through. Todd shares what he knows with the other passengers gathered around, but was still hoping to get in touch with Cindy to let her know that despite our previous plans, we never made it to the World Trade Center. He gets no answer and has to leave a voice mail.

Ken had heard Todd leaving a voice mail for Cindy to let her know that we were all safe. Todd indicated to her that Ken and Ty had not been able to get through and asked her, if she was able, would she mind calling Ken's wife Ginger, and in turn, have Ginger call June. Hopefully she would get the message soon. Thankfully for all of us, she did.

By this time, Cindy had landed in Greensboro, NC and is greeted by a cabin service employee who asked her if she'd heard the news.

"What news?" Cindy asked.

"The World Trade Center blew up!"

Another person hears their conversation, says that's not true, and that it was a plane that had flown into the towers. While they argue, Cindy shouted at them both, demanding to find out what's going on and still believing that we were there that morning. It would be a very anxious half hour or so before she discovered a voicemail. A voicemail that Todd had left earlier, indicating that we all were safe.

During the initial chaos of deplaning, Ken had tried to call his wife Ginger to let her know that he too was OK. Since he didn't have a cell phone, relatively new technology at the time, he tried one of the bank of pay phones that lined the wall nearby. Unfortunately for him and for Ty, who also didn't have a cell phone and was trying to call his wife June on a different pay phone, the only message they could get, if they were lucky enough to get a dial tone at all, was from an automated response.

"All circuits are busy now. Will you please try your call again later?"

After several tries and failures, both Ken and Ty walked back over to where Todd was sitting, leaving a voicemail message for his wife before Ken intervened and asked if she could try to get in touch with Ginger. Then Ty asked if Ginger would mind calling June. It had turned into an impromptu emergency chain phone call, but it would still be a while before everyone knew things were OK. Cindy was finally able to get through to Ginger, but getting through to June was a little more difficult.

Ty's wife June is an elementary school teacher and in such an environment, often there is an isolation, an insulation from the real world going on outside. While there may be television sets inside some schools, they are not usually used for actual network television viewing. They are used for closed-circuit, in-house programs or for watching DVDs. They are also not usually equipped with cable or satellite connectivity. It had what we used to refer to as "country cable" or "antennae TV", meaning one could only pick up the three major networks (ABC, CBS, NBC) and the public broadcasting system (PBS).

June had been teaching her students that morning, just like any other day, when she received a message to come to the school's front office. When she got there, she was given a note that had been phoned in from Ginger Harriss. It read: "Everything is fine. The guys are OK and they are safe."

June looked at the phone message again and was a little confused by the words. She had no idea of the day's events up to now.

"Well, why wouldn't they be?" she asked one of the secretaries.

Everyone in the office had already been informed of what was going on and was monitoring the situation through the television in the principal's back office, as well as through various phone calls and even a few parents who had come to pick up their kids early from school. The school staff had made sure that none of the other televisions in the building were to be turned on that day, so as not to scare the children. So June was more than just a little surprised when she found out what was going on, and more than relieved when she knew that none of us were there at heart of the tragedy. Shortly after that, she checked herself out of school for the rest of the day, knowing that she needed to go home to call Ty's mom, who knew that he was supposed to be there that day. She was able to get hold of Ty's mom relatively easy, then sat down to watch news coverage of the ongoing tragedy. What she saw after that, shook her and most all Americans to the core. Something we would find out soon enough from a young Pakistani cab driver.

5

Back in New York, the three of us sat in the gate area for the next half hour or so, hoping to gain more clarity on our situation. We began to watch the Airport Channel, which had been switched to live news coverage showing President George W. Bush at a school in Florida. Ty excuses himself to stretch his legs and go to the restroom. As he is in the restroom, he overhears a radio conversation between two airport employees that mentions the word "evacuation". Confident that they aren't discussing bodily functions, he then hears one of them say that he will walk the gate areas himself and instruct everyone where to go and what to do. With a little extra pep in his step, Ty makes a beeline back to where Ken and Todd are watching the President's initial remarks at the school event. Both men look at Ty, who is quickly approaching with eyes now as big as saucers, and has a slight look of urgency on his face and in his voice. He very quietly tells the other two to pick up their bags and start heading for the exit. As we are grabbing our things and making our way out, we noticed that our little group of new friends were now following us. Just about that time, the previously mentioned airport employee begins to calmly, but urgently tell everyone in our concourse to gather their belongings and evacuate the building. Not long after that, a public-address announcement was made for the entire airport, ordering the "calm" evacuation of all concourses. Occupants were asked to "calmly" proceed to the nearest public exit and leave the property. Calmly. As the three of us "calmly" trotted toward the exit, we formulated our plan. Ken would check the hotel phones for any vacancies and Todd and Ty would go outside to find a cab. Since we'd had a head start to the taxi stand, we figured we had a leg up on catching one, although we had no idea where we would go. We thought wrong. Outside, the cab stand line was already fifty people long! Ken then came outside only to give us more bad news. All the hotels were booked! So even if we did catch a cab, we had nowhere to go. We could see hundreds of people walking away from the airport toward the various hotels across the freeway. Many of those hotels had already been booked, but with nowhere else to go, most were hoping to camp out in the hotel lobby. We began to count heads in line and cabs remaining in the holding pen, and realized we were in trouble. It was going to be close. VERY close. Too close for our comfort. All the bridges TO the airport had been closed and were open only to take people AWAY from the airport. As each taxi loaded up each passenger and whisked them away, we knew that no additional cabs would be coming and there weren't enough left at the airport to take us...anywhere. Things were bleak.

At this point, we assumed we would find some place to rest and wait things out. Maybe one of the hotel lobbies or a fast food restaurant, since we weren't allowed back into the terminal or anywhere else on airport property. As we scouted out our planned walking departure, a small miracle happened. A small lady approached from the line in front of us and asked how many were in our party. Todd had to look down to reply.

"Three," he said.

She then asked three complete strangers (all men) if we wanted to share a cab with her. Seeing the bigger picture, she told us that she didn't want to get in a cab by herself because she thought it would be a waste. We had our doubts as we discussed it, but with Todd as our spokesman and deciding vote, we quickly agreed to share the cab. We promptly walked forward in the line with her, and the four of us got a cab. In fact, we climbed into the taxi introducing ourselves to her, as we heard the cab stand attendant in the background make an announcement that our taxi was the last cab available at LaGuardia. Everyone else behind us in line was out of luck and would have to walk. Since we were unsure of our destination, our tiny hero took on the role as spokeswoman as she told the driver her destination and the route she wanted him to take.

"The Bronx, please."

All three of us just looked at each other. We had been there only a few short hours ago, only to have our fun rained out. Now it seemed that the Bronx, or better yet, someone who lived in the Bronx, would be the one coming to the rescue of three Georgia boys. At any rate, we were going to the Bronx, one way or another.

Lauren Mishkin may only be five feet tall, but she's bigger than life to Ken Harriss, Todd Trainer, and Ty Wheeler. As we rode away from LaGuardia, Lauren explained that she, too, was trying to get to Atlanta, more specifically the northern suburb of Alpharetta. Her mom had a home there that they were getting ready to sell due to her poor health. Ty chimed in and told her that his pharmacy was on the Roswell/Alpharetta border, and Lauren knew exactly where it was. She went on to tell us that she was watching/listening to the three of us in the gate area. As events unfolded, her thoughts turned to her own sons, who travelled often on business and how she hoped that someone was taking care of them now. Because she was unable to help them, she thought she would help someone else's sons (once a parent, always a parent) and believed that we were the right ones. We are grateful to God that she felt that way.

We rode away and on our way out onto the Whitestone Expressway, we looked over our shoulders to see what was happening in lower

Manhattan. Ken was sitting in the back seat on the left side, trying to video the scene. It was easy to spot where the towers were, as huge clouds of smoke poured from the sky. However, with the cab moving in the opposite direction at a high rate of speed, plus other obstacles such as traffic, buildings, and trees obstructing the view, the video was very blurry and hard to see at best. The driver of the cab had the radio on, as the station was frantically delivering breaking news by the second. The North tower was burning and huge clouds of smoke and dust billowed where the South tower should have been. As the dust would later settle, it would reach a depth of a foot or more in most places. When we asked where the other tower was, our Pakistani cab driver managed to choke out five words.

"It fell. It just fell."

Dawn's Early Light

Ken and Todd at Times Square
September 10, 2001

Ken and Ty outside the subway station at
Radio City Music Hall
September 10, 2001

Dawn's Early Light

Riding the Subway to the Yankees game. Notice the WTC sign on the steel beam.

5:40 pm, September 10, 2001
A virtual monsoon at Yankee Stadium

Dawn's Early Light

Actor Jon Lovitz waiting out the rain delay
with Ty and Todd.

Smoke and ash rising from the remains of the World Trade
Center, September 11, 2001

The NYPD checking every car going into the city via the Hudson Parkway.

Michael and Lauren Mishkin
-Our Heroes-

Dawn's Early Light

At Penn Station, awaiting the train that would take us home - or reasonably close to home.

Ty and Todd exiting the train in Richmond, Virginia for the last leg of the trip home.

Dawn's Early Light

...With Ken not far behind!

One year later, the return.
May 3, 2002
The Cross in the center of it all.

Dawn's Early Light

Dawn's Early Light

Michael S. Mishkin
Chief Executive Officer

New York Office
875 Avenue of the Americas
New York, NY 10001
Tel   212.695.7495 ext. 25
Fax 212.695.7260

Atlanta Office
12850 Highway 9
Suite 600-133
Alpharetta, GA 30004
Tel   770.442.9775
Fax 770.777.8226

mike@quotopia.com
www.quotopia.com

```
DL RECORD LOCATOR W8F5GR
  1.8/01WHEELER/TYRONEK**073225700-68
  2.8/01HARRISS/KENNETHE**073225700-69
  3.8/01TRAINER/RUSSELLTODD**073225700-01
 1 DL 708F 10SEP1 ATLEWR MM3    640A  845A
 2 DL1288F 11SEP2 EWRATL MM3    635A  859A
HA FAX- ** SSRS PRESENT **
```

Dawn's Early Light

```
NY0910   BX 215    B    4      COMP
  EVENT CODE    SECTION/BOX   ROW   SEAT    All Taxes Incl. if Applicable
$   0.00  MAIN BOX SEC 3      ADM.$
PRICE & ALL TAXES INCL.
                        RAIN CHECK
  BX 215         YANKEE STADIUM
  SECTION/BOX
  CA 132X     PRICE INCL. CITY/ST TAX
   B    4       NEW YORK YANKEES
  ROW   SEAT
  YAN524C       VS BOSTON RED SOX
 31MAR01   MON SEP 10, 2001 7:05PM
```

```
         Riders        AMTRAK       Baggage
                         1
              Name of Guest
           WHEELER/TYRONE

           NEW YORK PENN, NY
           RICHMOND, VA
            Carrier     Train         Date
           2V   95              13SEP01
            YD       Space/Car
                 RESERVD COACH
         Form of Payment
         AP    2559631420398    DS
           Rail Fare                 Account Charge
                 $78.00                 $.00
           Fare Plans                  Total
                                     $78.00
         BOTC
           Ticket Num
           2564829074817        01  No. 01
           Date Issued                Ticket Condition
           13SEP01              131D07
                       GUEST RECEIPT
```

6

"So where do we go from here?" we silently think to ourselves. Well, our new friend Lauren lived with her husband Michael in the Bronx, and as our cab ride continued through the northern end of Manhattan toward their home, she suggested that we can regroup and make alternate travel plans at their house. After all, her husband would already be there and he could help us with our new arrangements.

A normally short ride ended up taking a couple of hours because of all the people on the road. We listened in disbelief and horror as reporters describe the collapse of the south tower, just out of our sight as we headed north. Finally, we arrived at Lauren's apartment building and head inside, the three of us slightly overwhelmed at this point. We took a special elevator to the top floor of the building, Lauren's home, only to find out that her husband Michael is not there. She shows us around the townhouse, as the perfect hostess would, and introduces us to her husband's sports memorabilia collection. This is no small collection---it's an entire room of things hung on the walls and dozens of boxes of photos, bats, balls, jerseys, and rare baseball cards, many of which were autographed by the athletes represented. Don't forget that the three of us are obviously pretty big sports fans ourselves (especially Ty, who has quite a bit of memorabilia himself, and Ken, who was part-owner of a small sports collectibles shop). We are all thinking we're about to make a serious sports connection with Lauren's husband.

The phone rings. It's Michael Mishkin, checking in to make sure his wife is safe. Lauren says that she's fine and is home now, but she has brought a few new friends home because they had nowhere else to go. He's not particularly thrilled to find out its three <u>men</u>, so he reminded her not to show them the sports room. Too late!

His other piece of news is that he's just a few miles away checking up on Lauren's mother. Her caregivers believe that she might have had a stroke and he suggested that she come to the hospital. After Lauren shared this with us, we decided that we should leave and try to find a hotel nearby, but she insists that we stay. She even goes so far as to show us where the towels are and how to work the TV remote. She gives us the number to a local pizza place, direction to the deli right down the street, and even tries to give us money to make sure we're in good shape to make it through the day.

Suddenly, a flood of emotions began to rain down on each of us. We now began to realize the gravity of our situation and just how different this day could have been---and very nearly was---for us. We are keenly aware of God's presence, protection, and provision at this moment, and Todd asked Lauren if it's OK to pray with her before she leaves. She agreed and we stood, holding hands in her hallway, thanking God for the ways He has shown Himself faithful that morning, asking for help for the victims and first responders, and asking for healing for Lauren's mother.

*****

Meanwhile, back in Woodstock, Ty's wife June watched on TV as the towers fell, but a flurry of activity had already been set into motion at the church the three men attended, the First Baptist

Church of Woodstock, Georgia.

Every Tuesday, the staff of the church held a prayer breakfast before starting work. Usually the mini-service was led by either the Senior Pastor, Dr. Johnny Hunt or the Senior Associate Pastor, Jim Law. However, on this particular Tuesday, Pastor Johnny was on a sabbatical and had gone out to Springdale, Arkansas with his wife Janet to visit his daughter and son-in-law, who were working with a local church there. Pastor Jim was also out of town, having flown out to Las Vegas, Nevada to check up on the progress of one of the new church plants that Woodstock had helped to start. That left the prayer breakfast to be led by either Senior Staff Member and business manager Dan Dorner or Bill Kelley, who was in charge of the prayer ministry. They talked and came to an agreement that Bill would lead the service that morning. Everything that morning seem like a normal Tuesday morning until Bill got ready to speak. That was when Senior Staff Member Neil Brown whispered in his ear that a plane had hit one of the twin towers. Well, as you can imagine, they immediately began to pray about the situation, thinking like most others that it was a small commuter-type plane. It was not until ten minutes later that they realized that it was a large plane, so the staff made a decision to break up the prayer breakfast a little early. Some retreated to their office or to previously scheduled appointments, but most gathered around a television in the B building café of the church to watch the unfolding news, including the leveling of the second tower.

Word had already spread that several church members and pastors were either flying out of town that morning, had relatives in New York City, or were actually in New York City. Linda Holland, the church's switchboard operator, was overwhelmed with the number of calls. Meanwhile, Bill was called into Dan's office, where they decided that they would open up the church that night for an official prayer service. Some people had already made an executive decision on their own, as several church members, deeply burdened for our country and for the situations of other church members, had already begun to trickle in to pray. Pastor Johnny had also called in to say that he would join the prayer service by phone since he was stranded in Arkansas. Not long after that, the church sent out an email blast and text message (for those who had it at the time) to all its members, alerting them that an official House of Prayer service would take place at 7:00 p.m. later that night.

While 7:00 p.m. may have been the official starting time for the prayer service, Bill, Dan, and Minister of Music Scott White were not surprised to see many people there early, already on their faces at the altar, lifting our country up to God. Also, not surprisingly the sanctuary, which held nearly 3,000 seats, was filled to capacity. Scott led the worship music that night, then Bill and several others prayed for our country. They prayed for friends and relatives, emergency and hospital personnel, and first responders in New York, Washington DC, and Pennsylvania. Later, Pastor Johnny joined the service by phone and was linked into the sound system so he could address the entire church and lift up more prayers. After reassuring the congregation that he was OK and that we all would be OK, he focused his prayers on a few different areas. He prayed that this would be a revival of sorts, an awakening of the church, <u>His</u> church, as we unified together in crying out to God and reaffirming our total dependence on Him alone. He lifted up our enemies and those who'd carried out these terrible atrocities on our citizens. Lastly, he lifted up those who were stranded and scattered around the country, and in New York City specifically. Many of those were from his own congregation, including Ken, Todd, and Ty. The prayer service would last until at least 8:30 p.m., but once again several members stayed later to lift their burdens to the Lord.

*****

Even before he'd hung up, Pastor Johnny Hunt had a longing to be with those in his congregation, and everyone felt the same way toward him. He knew in his heart and soul that he wanted and needed to be there, but he was stranded in Arkansas with no flights going to Atlanta anytime soon. It was earlier that day when he remembered his partner in ministry and best friend Jim Law was also stuck in Las Vegas, waiting to get back home. Since there were no flights going anywhere, renting a car was the only option. Most folks who could get a rental car at the airport or anywhere else had already scarfed them up, but Jim had an inside contact. He knew a gentleman based in Orlando, Florida that was a regional manager with one of the larger rental car companies, so he took a chance and called him. The regional manager said that he'd gladly do him that favor, but that they only had one or two cars remaining in Las Vegas, and they were smaller cars. Jim replied that he'd take one, but that he'd have to leave the car in Atlanta, due to the current situation. After they'd gotten everything worked out, Pastor Johnny called Jim and told him to pick up the Hunts in Arkansas on his way through. Shortly after, Jim climbed into a small, cramped rental car and drove all night from Las Vegas to Springdale, stopping only for gas and food. Scooping up the Hunts and alternating drivers along the way, the trio made it as far south as Tupelo, Mississippi before grabbing a hotel and spending the night there. They would make it back to Georgia the next day, but some people were still stranded in New York City, desperate to get home. Home to Woodstock.

7

Home.

Most of the time, the word evokes pleasant memories. Whether from our past or our present, it often serves as a source of comfort. A source of strength. A source of safety. A source of togetherness.

Home alone.

Those two words have a totally different connotation and conjure up very different, contrasting images.

Ken Harriss. Todd Trainer. Ty Wheeler.

We were together, but we were alone.

Home alone. In someone else's home.

The three of us did what most everyone else did that day---we watched the news. We speculated. We shed tears. We prayed. We were justifiably angry. Still, we knew we were exactly where we were supposed to be, when we were supposed to be there.

The Mishkin's apartment patio covered nearly half of the roof of their building, and what a spectacular view it had! Looking southward, we could see the smoldering cloud of dust in lower Manhattan, mere remains of what had once been there earlier in the day. The black oily smoke would continue to hang over the city for many days to come. No airplanes soared overhead except for the Navy fighter jets flying a protective grid pattern over New York City. To the west side, we could see the Henry Hudson Parkway snaking its way south and the Hudson River just beyond that. The southbound side of the parkway was at a complete standstill, as all traffic into the city had been halted. The only vehicles being allowed through were emergency vehicles. We watched as hundreds of ambulances, fire and rescue trucks, and police cars, many of which came from other states farther north than New York, made it through traffic and past the roadblocks. Most of the fire trucks were filled to capacity with firefighters, many riding on top carrying large American flags. If you happened to live anywhere north of New York City that day and needed emergency services, you might have been out of luck.

*****

In the meantime, Lauren has arrived at the hospital to check up on her mother and is greeted by Michael, who assumes out loud that she has sent the three strangers packing. She tells him that she left us back in their apartment. As he protests and insists that these three men will have stolen everything they have and leave them with an empty apartment, Lauren calmly reassures her husband.

"They can't be too bad---they prayed for me!"

As it turned out, Lauren and Michael would be at the hospital all day.

Back in the Bronx, our only trip out of the apartment complex that afternoon was to get something to eat. As all men do when they're out of town, we went to the nearby store and purchased the barest of food essentials, meaning we ate chips and cookies, and drank sodas all afternoon. It was here where we learned of the cookie that was a New York staple, but not found as much in the South. At least as big as a grapefruit without any of its nutritional value, it is classified as a cookie, but it eats more like a cake---with lots of frosting. Vanilla <u>and</u> chocolate frosting! On the outside, it looked very similar to the Chinese Yin Yang symbol. While its name is not very clever, the three of us became expert connoisseurs of black-and-whites in quick order. It still may be the best cookie we've ever eaten, or at least in the top two or three. As an old football coach once said, "If it's not in a class of its own, it sure don't take long to call the roll."

Around 9:00 p.m. or so that night, we discovered that we were truly hungry for some real food, so we thought we'd try another New York favorite, pizza. New York's pizza is different from other types of pizza in that the slices are longer and thinner, yet just as tasty as regular pizza or Chicago-style pizza, which is a thicker, deep-dish pan pizza with the sauce on top. All are excellent in their own right, the best one depending on where you're from or just personal preference. We thought we'd try to order from the pizza place just down the street that Lauren had recommended. We decided to have it delivered instead of walking over to pick it up since we didn't want to leave the news coverage. Todd called the pizza place and when he gave out the delivery address to the man on the other end of the line, he got an unexpected response.

"Hold on a minute, your dad's here."

Todd is momentarily stunned as the pizza guy hands the phone to the mystery man on the line.

"Hello, who is this?" Todd asked.

"This is Michael Mishkin. Who are you?"

The Mishkins had stopped by the pizza shop at the exact same moment we were ordering to pick up dinner for us on their way home from the hospital. As Todd explained who he was and that he was one of the three men his wife had left in their home, his reply was what we learned later as a classic, typical Michael Mishkin response.

"Well, do I have any furniture left?"

Just a few minutes later, the Mishkins walk in the door with dinner. We finally get to meet Michael, who is as tall as his wife is---vertically challenged.

Instantly, any anxiety or awkwardness we were feeling was dissipated by his calm nature and gentle spirit. It didn't hurt that he was as much of a sports fanatic and junk food junkie as we were, although Lauren had done her best to curtail the junk food. We ate dinner together and got to know each other better before each of us found a place in their home to rest for the night. For the next two days, the Mishkins treated us like family. They still do today.

The next day was a Wednesday, and having known us for less than twenty-four hours, the Mishkins still trusted us enough to leave us alone again in their apartment while they went to check on Lauren's mom. Later on that day, we went downstairs to get some fresh air. Outside, we stood and watched as more rescuers and their equipment made their way south again. By this time, the Port Authority Police were allowing just one vehicle through their roadblock at a time, but only after a search of the vehicle and all occupants. September in New York City is still hot and these guys were roasting in the sun for hours on end. We'd learned from our pastor that "we are never more like Jesus than when we are giving". It seemed to simultaneously pop into our heads, so we decided we needed to do something. Sitting around all day accomplished us nothing, so we did what many others had already done before us and would do after us. We served those who served us.

The three of us made our way to the store again and bought as much water and snacks as we could carry to the Port Authority Police working the roadblock. It was strange being able to walk right up onto a normally busy freeway and serve these men and women the only way we know how at the time. We know it was a small part in a bigger play, but we were happy and honored to do it, knowing that we literally gave a cup of cold water to those folks in His name.

*****

For almost three days, the Mishkins would take care of us, taking us to dinner and continuing our newly-found love affair with deli meats, New York-style pizza, and black-and-white cookies. Now that he'd gotten to know us, Michael had grown to like us and was glad to keep us around. However, we ate so poorly that Lauren accused him of keeping us around so he could eat the junk food he normally wasn't allowed to eat! Through Michael's work connections, Todd's dad back in Atlanta, and our regular dosage of news, we continued to check each source as to if and when airports or rental car agencies would reopen. Things were not looking very promising as we gathered information and continued to check the internet. Finally, late on Wednesday afternoon we caught our break. No planes or car rentals were available, but they'd opened up the railways. Well, at least some of them. Amtrak had opened up a few of its lines, but none went as far South as Atlanta. The closest we would be able to get would be a run from New York City to Richmond, Virginia. Thursday afternoon would be the earliest we would be able to leave---by train. We purchased three tickets on the Amtrak website, plunking down our $78.00 each for a one-way ticket and sat back, praying that we'd be able to make it out.

8

Thursday, September 13th. None of us are superstitious, but after the luck we'd had, we are glad the calendar didn't read Friday the 13th. We needed all the luck---and prayer---we could get on this day. By now, some of the highways and parkways were slowly beginning to reopen little by little. Michael had found out that the route that he would take to his office at Avenue of the Americas was open. As Chief Executive Officer of Quotopia, he knew he'd have to put in a few hours at work just to make sure any possible glitches in his business would be kept to a minimum. He offered to drop us off at the nearest Amtrak station on his way. We quickly agreed and made our plans to head South. Todd had called his dad to let him know what we were doing and when our scheduled departure from New York City and hopeful arrival in Richmond would be. His dad had then called Todd's younger brother Tony, who also lived in the metro Atlanta area, and together they agreed to drive a van to Richmond to pick us up and bring us the rest of the way home.

We said our bittersweet goodbyes to Lauren, and loaded up our stuff into Michael's car. Traffic heading toward Penn Station was lighter than usual, since all roads still weren't open and people were staying off the ones that were open if they didn't have to be out. Dropping us off at the station, we shook hands and thanked Michael profusely, then sprinted downstairs. We'd gotten this far and we were eager to catch our train. No way were we going to miss it, unless something unforeseen happened and the route was cancelled. A short time later, we boarded the 95 train for a six-hour trip toward home on the Northeast Regional. It connected several sites up and down the eastern seaboard, and was an interesting way to see parts of several states one wouldn't normally see since most travel done here is usually through the air. We rolled through parts of Newark and the New Jersey Meadowlands, near the edges of Pennsylvania and Delaware, down through Maryland, and dissecting the heart of Virginia. The coach seats were fairly comfortable, but during the last parts of the trip through small town, rural Virginia, we all were starting to grow tired and restless. That last stretch of track down into Richmond gave us plenty of time to think about everything we'd been through in the previous two or three days. That only added to the exhaustion we were all beginning to feel. As our journey reached its halfway point a few minutes later, we grabbed our stuff and disembarked once the train had pulled into the Richmond station. Ty's last memory of Richmond was watching Ken bound over the several sets of train tracks we had to cross to get to the station platform, though Ken said he was worried that Todd and Ty were walking so fast that they'd leave him in Richmond! Within a few minutes, Todd had summoned his dad, who'd been waiting nearby, by cellphone. One of the best sights we saw on that whole trip was the sight of Mr. Wendel Trainer and his son Tony pulling up in the van. We all grabbed our things and climbed into the van, each one of us planting ourselves on our own bench seat row in the vehicle. After introductions, we all proceeded to tell our story, most of it voiced by Todd since his dad and brother were the audience. It must've been the adrenaline or just the retelling of our story that kept our attention in the waning daylight as our van headed South on Interstate 85. As we traded updates and shared stories, it was almost a cathartic experience as we travelled past shopping malls, historical sites, and race tracks, unloading our thoughts and emotions as we went. Before we'd gotten out of North Carolina, our talking had slowed and fatigue had started to replace the anxiety. Soon after, all three of us were dead asleep, except for Todd in fits and starts, leaving Mr. Wendel and Tony to get us through the night and back to Atlanta. As the van crawled into the suburbs of metro Atlanta in the wee hours, the freeway lights roused us from our sleep, letting us know that we were almost there.

Home again.

Finally.

*****

When the next day dawned, there we were. All back in our homes, our own beds, with our own families. All having to relive our tales of near misses and what could have beens. In addition to our families, there was also the consideration of our employers. We'd only intended to be gone for

Monday and Tuesday. Only two days of work wouldn't be putting us too far behind. Until the two days stretched into five days. Not that we could help it mind you, but missing a whole week's worth of work? Well, that could set you back for a while, especially for someone like Ken, who owns his own business. Friday would prove to be not very productive for all of us, as most co-workers and friends were begging to hear details of our story. They knew a lot of the basic parts of the story, as they had been praying for us the whole time, but now they wanted specifics. We were tired, but we were all too glad to tell them of our good fortune and how only God could have sustained us through everything that we experienced.

Todd had gone in a little later than he normally would have on a Friday. Still exhausted from our long ordeal, he relayed our tale to all of his co-workers, then settled in and tried to catch up on his work. Not long after, his boss, Bob Hester, called him into his office, where he prayed with Todd and for Cindy, who still had not made it home. He immediately set Todd's mind at ease and was more than compassionate in making sure Todd was in the right frame of mind to come back to work.

Cindy would not make it home from Greensboro until the next day (Saturday), safe and sound. We had driven right by her hotel on our way home from Richmond, but she still had to stay there to bring the plane home to Atlanta once the airspace had opened up. They enjoyed a VERY long hug when she walked through the door.

Ken went in on that Friday with a slight sense of dread, knowing that several of his drywall projects would be behind or delayed, not the thing a business owner wants to hear. However, his business partner was in good shape physically, had understood the gravity of the situation, and had stepped in to help until Ken could get back into town. A lot of projects had gotten delayed anyway due to the circumstances surrounding 9/11, so Ken was in much better shape than he thought he would ever be.

Ty was the luckiest one of the three. Originally, he was scheduled to only work Wednesday and

Thursday, September 12th and 13th, because that was his short week rotation on the pharmacy schedule. Well, that obviously didn't happen because of being stuck in New York, but he'd gotten word to his wife, who in turn, had gotten word to his pharmacy partners and the scheduling coordinator. They'd covered the store for him almost immediately. When he'd gotten up on Friday, he drove over to work, where he ran into two of the people who'd been praying for him. One of his pharmacy partners was there and hugged him, insisting that he didn't have to pay back the days he was previously scheduled to work. The other was a technician from the small island nation of Trinidad and Tobago, who also bear-hugged him and even shed a tear or two. After he briefly told them his New York story, Ty went home and caught up on other errands and phone calls.

So many people wanted to hear our story that they would ask one of the three of us, then later call the other two to hear their version of the story, so as not to miss one tiny detail. Our church family was so great in checking up on us, and especially praying for us by name in the prayer services. In the back of our minds, we wondered why we don't realize how much God's hand is on our everyday lives until things like this happen. I remember our Minister of Music, Scott White, marveled at our story and then the first words he uttered once our story ended.

"God spared your life."

He didn't say it for shock value, or to be overly dramatic or melodramatic. He meant it with all his heart, and the more we thought about it, the more we knew how right he was. As members of his choir and good friends with him also, we knew his heart and how he had been praying for us. Everyone had. People were <u>still</u> flocking to the church on their way to pray, but Sunday was on the way.

The prayer that occurred during the week had been filling churches all over the nation like a giant revival, even if there was not an officially organized service. Houses of worship were near or at capacity all over. Ours was no different as Sunday morning rolled around. First Baptist Church Woodstock was packed as people came together as one. Citizens.

Patriots. Christians and non-Christians. We were united in our patriotism, our tears, and our prayer. Even if no one remembered a word that day, we were all one body, one voice that prayed for those who wished to do us harm. Praying for our enemies, and those that longed to carry out their evil desires against America and its citizens was a common theme that day. Yet, as the choir began to sing a special song, several in the sanctuary and in the choir burst into tears, including Ty, who had to sit down during the special music. Finally, the grief of everything they had been through had simply overwhelmed him. He was not alone on that day.

9

The timeline of our story is still somewhat unbelievable to this day. Our trip started in the wee morning hours, the dawn's early light, in Atlanta, Georgia on September 10th, 2001, continued in New York City, and was supposed to have ended in Atlanta on the evening of September 11th. Who knew that we'd end up sleeping in a stranger's home in the Bronx the same night we should have returned to our own homes? No one but God. With some help from Time/Life Inc., the timeline for that day's events is as follows:

8:47 a.m.—American Airlines Flight 11 from Boston to Los Angeles crashes into the North Tower (1 World Trade Center).

9:02 a.m.—United Airlines Flight 175 from Boston to Los Angeles crashes into the South Tower (2 World Trade Center).

9:07 a.m.—All New York City airports are shut down.

9:08 a.m.—The Federal Aviation Administration (FAA) closes all New York Area airports.

9:21 a.m.—All bridges and tunnels in New York are closed.

9:26 a.m.—All non-military planes are grounded and all flights in the United States are cancelled.

9:50 a.m.—The South Tower (Tower 2) collapses.

10:28 a.m.—The North Tower (Tower 1) collapses.

Less than two hours after the first crash, both towers (110 stories) collapse. Around 2:30 p.m. that afternoon, it was announced that there would be no commercial air traffic until noon on Wednesday at the earliest. When all is said and done, over 3,000 are reported to be dead, more than either Pearl Harbor or D-Day.

For many, our story may seem fairly anti-climactic. All of the drama, if you will, is at the beginning of the story. The drama of that day was the catalyst for an entire spectrum of emotions for every

American. In the early morning hours, the dawn's early light of that day, pure evil boarded several separate airlines in the Northeastern part of the United States with deadly intentions and maximum destruction on its collective mind. This country and its citizens still bear the scars inflicted by the hands of cowards we call terrorists. We would never dream of minimizing the events of September 11th, 2001 by cramming a few otherwise boring details about us into the awful nature of other's tragedy and their true reality story. Many people gave everything that day and never made it home. We are constantly reminded that their friends and family members still grieve openly, and with raw pain, when recounting that horrible day. Our hearts ache with them, and we ask God for healing in their lives.

For Ken Harriss, Todd Trainer, and Ty Wheeler, that clear blue sky Tuesday could have gone very differently---but it didn't. In fact, with all things considered, it ended as well as could be expected. We were <u>NOT</u> able to stay an extra day in New York City because flights with open seats mysteriously filled up in a span of just a few hours.

We were <u>NOT</u> in a restaurant at the World Trade Center eating breakfast like we'd planned when the attacks occurred. We were <u>NOT</u> on a plane commandeered by a terrorist coward and we were <u>NOT</u> on a plane that needed to be grounded mid-flight. We were <u>NOT</u> left walking away from the airport with no plan regarding where to go because one particular stranger reached out to us. We were <u>NOT</u> left alone because that stranger saw in us her own children and desired to make our circumstances a little easier. We were <u>NOT</u> alone because God was with us.

    She was on the Atlanta flight that day because her son lived there and she wanted to visit him and her grandchildren before taking care of some other business matters. Lauren Mishkin had spent some of her youth in Georgia and at heart, just might be a Georgia peach. Marriage and other matters had led to her transplant to New York, thus giving her the best of both worlds, North and South. She noticed us at the airport because we seemed to be having fun and were "behaving" ourselves, being courteous and respectful of others. Eventually, Michael and Lauren would move to the Atlanta area for a while, but have recently moved to the south Florida area. During their time here, our families were able to see the Mishkins several times and develop a great relationship. Even if we don't see them for months, we still speak with them each September 11th. That was a really tough day for them also. They lost friends when the towers fell, yet still found the time to selflessly impact our lives.

We know that there are thousands of stories out there just like ours, and we love hearing all of them, especially when the storyteller mentions the compassion they felt that day. For us though, this story is not anti-climactic. September 11th is a day that still brings back difficult memories, but the lessons we learned that day are far from tragic. September 11th, 2001 is the day that God showed Himself to be very real in our lives. Apart from the day each of us became a Christian, we've never once felt His presence like we did on that day. Many have asked where God was on that day and how He could have allowed something like that to happen. We are convinced that He was right where He is today---still on His throne.

For the most part, none of us are conspiracy theorists, so we hope that this story does not prompt that kind of debate. However, we do believe that evil exists when God is absent from the hearts of men. There are those who seek to do harm to those by whom they feel threatened, but God promises that He will use for good and for His glory what others have meant for harm. God showed up and showed Himself to be strong and faithful through the words, actions, and hearts of millions of people that day. For Ken, Todd, and Ty, He proved His presence through the peace they experienced in the midst of tragedy. He displayed His providence in knowing what the future would hold. He granted protection in changing our plans to keep us from harm. He poured out His provision through the lives of (formerly) perfect strangers. We are thankful that sometimes, despite our objections, His ways are not our ways and His plans are not our plans.

So you see, that's the real climax of our story. God is who He says He is, and He will do what He says He will do. He is both Creator and Ruler of all. Nothing happens to us that isn't filtered through His fingers first. When He makes a promise to us, you can rest assuredly in the knowledge that He will keep it. As a child of God, you are **NEVER** outside of His reach, and you are **NEVER** not on His mind. However, the real question involves your availability to His reach and His thoughts. Do you know Him? I mean **REALLY** know Him, not just know **OF** Him. He desires to know you in an intimate way, to live in your heart and be the Light, **YOUR** Light, in an otherwise dark world. He has made this possible only because of the sacrifice He willingly made through His Son, not only on our behalf, but on your behalf too if you trust and believe in Him. Our prayer is that if you don't know Him and how He can transform your life for the better, that you will seek Him first before you seek all the things you might think He gives. If you want to know how to do that or if you just aren't sure you've got it 100% correct, please reach out to any of us mentioned in this story and we'll talk. Thanks for sticking with our story to the end, and know that we love you all very much. God bless you!

EPILOGUE

Just because I know some folks are wondering, and also to the point that it helps tie up one of the few loose ends in our story, we eventually were able to go back to New York City to finish our trip. Since the New York Yankees game on September 10th, 2001 against the Boston Red Sox had been rained out, the Yankees issued an announcement that our rain check tickets could be used for any remaining non-Red Sox game in 2001 or for any number of select games in 2002. There were not that many games left in the 2001 season, plus our schedules would not allow for a return visit so soon after this one, so we made the decision to come back in 2002. Looking back on it now, I don't know that we'd have wanted to come back, even if we could, mere days after the tragedy. Even a little over a month later, Ty was still a little apprehensive in boarding a flight to Argentina for a mission trip he'd planned with the church.

The three of us got together later and decided that our new choice would be Friday, May 3, 2002 against the Seattle Mariners. We were able to fly out again on buddy passes thanks to Todd and Cindy, arriving in New York City just after the morning rush hour. We checked into the same hotel as before and spent our day sightseeing, as well as sampling some of New York's finest pizza, cheesecake, and black-and-whites. We rode the subway over to the stadium early so that we could see Monument Grove and other things we'd been unable to see during the rained-out game the year before. This time, the weather was great and although the Yankees lost to the Mariners 6-2, we still had a great time and were able to fulfill our dream of attending a game at Yankee Stadium.

However, before we left New York the next day, which was on a Saturday night, we had one more place we wanted to visit. A somber visit to the site where the Twin Towers once stood. The makeshift memorials were still surrounding the chain link fences months later. Flowers, pictures, personal articles from some victims, flyers, concrete memorials, and signs took up almost every inch of space available. Patriotic emblems and Bible verses were the prevalent themes, and we all made sure we got photos of these and with each other in front of them. Like most Americans, our patriotism and our pride in America in how we responded as a nation to the tragedy was never more passionate. Inside the chain link fences, there wasn't very much to see, just a huge crater that was littered with debris to be removed and newer construction that was beginning. Much of Ground Zero was roped off, so we weren't able to really see a great deal. It didn't matter. In our minds, it was, in a sense, a sort of closure to the whole ordeal. It made our story a little more personal, a little more real to each of us, and gave us an even better perspective on those who gave everything they had on that fateful day, including their lives. The one thing that we were able to see and that stood out among the ruins there was the symbol of all that keeps us and sustains us, even today. The one thing that makes life worth living and the symbolic reason we will have everlasting life. The twenty-foot piece of two intersecting steel beams. Two steel beams in the shape of a cross.

Made in the USA
Columbia, SC
13 September 2024